W9-AOK-186

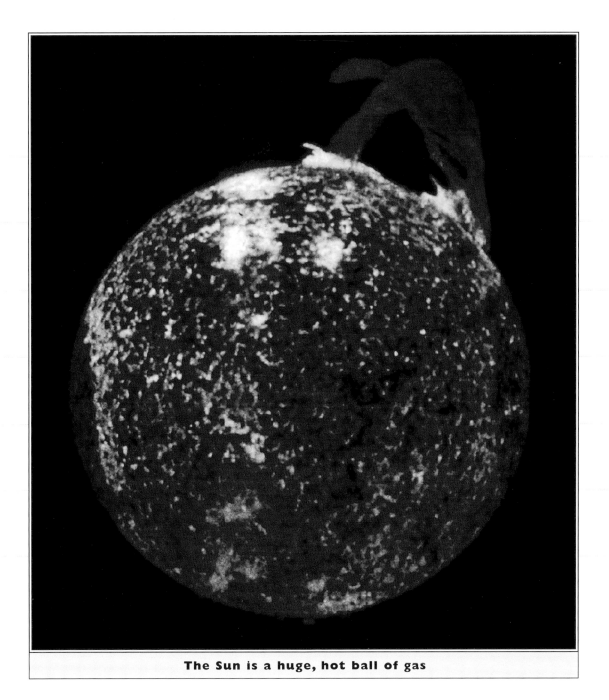

The Sun is a huge, hot ball of gas

THE Sun

Steve Potts

A⁺

Smart Apple Media

COPYRIGHT

☀ Published by Smart Apple Media

1980 Lookout Drive, North Mankato, MN 56003

Designed by Rita Marshall

Copyright © 2002 Smart Apple Media. International copyright reserved in all countries. No part of this book may be reproduced in any form without written permission from the publisher.

Printed in the United States of America

☀ Photographs by Tom Stack & Associates (JPL, NASA, NOAA, Brian Parker, TSADO)

☀ Library of Congress Cataloging-in-Publication Data

Potts, Steve. The sun / by Steve Potts. p. cm. — (Our solar system series)

Includes bibliographical references and index.

☀ ISBN 1-58340-092-3

1. Sun—Juvenile literature. [1. Sun.] I. Title.

QB521.5 .P68 2001   523.7—dc21   2001020121

☀ First Edition 9 8 7 6 5 4 3 2 1

THE Sun

CONTENTS

The Sun's Heat

The universe contains billions of galaxies. A galaxy is a group of stars, planets, moons, dust, gas, and other objects in space held together by **gravity**. Our galaxy, the Milky Way, has more than 100 billion stars. Stars are very large, hot balls of gas. One of these stars, the Sun, is the center of our solar system. The Sun is 100 times the diameter of Earth and weighs 740 times the total weight of all nine planets in our solar system. The Sun can be broken down into six parts. The

Our Sun is a "dwarf star" compared to other stars

center of the Sun is called the core. The layer above the core

is the radiation zone. The outer part of the Sun's interior is

called the convection zone. Above the convection zone is the

photosphere. This is the part of the Sun that **The Sun is**

big enough

can be seen from Earth. It is the Sun's lower **to hold**

more than

atmosphere. ☀ Above the photosphere is **a million**

planets the

the chromosphere. The outermost layer of the **size of Earth.**

Sun is the corona. The corona extends millions of miles into

space and is a million times fainter than the photosphere. ☀

The temperature at the Sun's core is 27 million degrees F

(15 million degrees C). The Sun's outer layers cool down to

9,900° F (5,500° C) before sending energy into space.

The Sun's photosphere is visible to the naked eye

The corona is the Sun's faint, outermost layer

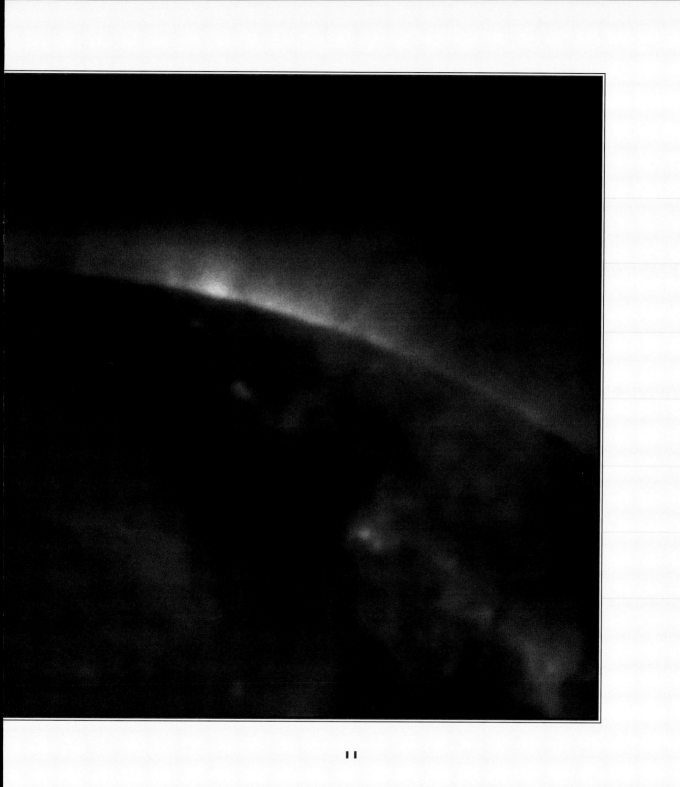

Sunspots

The Sun's **atmosphere** is very thick. It rises millions of miles into space from the Sun's surface. This atmosphere is 73 percent hydrogen and 25 percent helium. The Sun has very little oxygen in its atmosphere. It would be impossible for any form of life as we know it to survive on the Sun's surface.

The Sun gives off 40,000 watts of light from every square inch of its surface.

☀ When scientists began studying the Sun with telescopes, they were surprised to find a group of dark areas on the surface. They called these areas sunspots. ☀ These spots, which

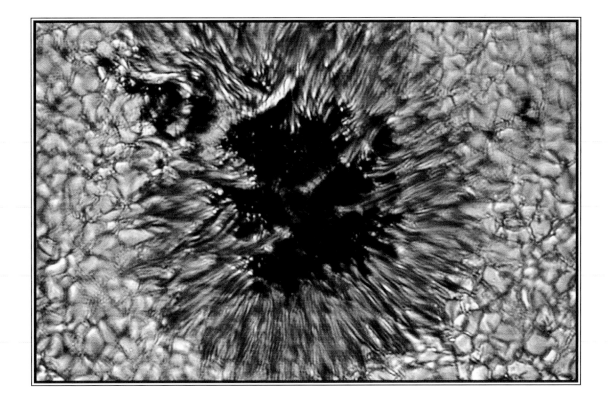

don't remain in the same place for very long, cause **magnetic**

fields to form beneath the Sun's surface. When spots erupt on

the Sun, they can interfere with radio communications on Earth.

A close-up view of a sunspot

This is because sunspots send magnetic energy into space. ☀

Scientists believe sunspots may also impact weather on Earth.

In the 1600s, there was a period when there were few sunspots.

Temperatures in northern Europe dropped several degrees.

The Corona

In 1962, scientists detected something called solar wind.

This wind comes from the Sun's corona and travels at speeds

between 185 and 435 miles (300–700 km) per second. ☀

The Sun's corona contains electrically charged gas called plas-

ma. It is this plasma which is thrown from the Sun, beyond

Earth and into deep space. The corona and the faint glow of

solar wind is visible to the naked eye during a solar eclipse.

☀ The Moon completes its **orbit** of Earth every 27 days.

Plasma erupting from the Sun's corona

During its orbit, the Moon will sometimes pass between the Sun and Earth, blocking out the sunlight. This is a solar eclipse. Around the world, there are between two and five solar eclipses visible every year. Most of them do not last more than a few minutes.

☀ Even though the corona is a million times dimmer than the center of the Sun, it

Certain areas of the Sun's corona that contain less plasma are called coronal holes.

is very dangerous for humans to look directly at it, even during a total eclipse. Reflecting the Sun off a mirror and onto a

A ring, or halo, can appear around the Sun in winter

piece of paper is the best way to view an eclipse. ☀

Thousands of years ago, people feared eclipses. Some still do.

They saw them as warnings of bad things to come. The Shang

people of ancient China believed that during a solar eclipse, a monster was eating the sun. The word "eclipse" in their

language meant "eat."

Earth's Sun

As Earth rotates around the Sun, it also tilts on its

axis. When the northern hemisphere is tilted toward the Sun,

it experiences summer. When it's tilted away from the Sun, it

experiences winter. Earth takes 365 days, or one full year,

to complete its orbit around the Sun. ☀ The Sun,

like many stars, has a life span of about 10 billion years.

All life on Earth relies on energy from the Sun

Astronomers calculate that the Sun is now about 4.6 billion years old. They predict that when the Sun reaches the end of its life, in about five billion years, it will explode and destroy the solar system. ☀ There is still much we do not know and do not understand about the Sun. But as new technologies are developed to help us explore it, we will come to know more of its secrets.

Without the Sun's electro-magnetic radiation, Earth would be completely dark.

Bursts of electrically charged gas are called flares

The Sun can turn the sky into a work of art

INFORMATION

Index

Words to Know

atmosphere—the nearly invisible layer of gases that surrounds a planet

axis—a non-moving, imaginary line that an object rotates around

gravity—a force that attracts all objects in the universe; it's the force that makes things fall to the ground

magnetic fields—forces released from a planet or star that are caused by certain movements of electrical currents or electrically charged particles

orbit—a repeating circular pattern of one object traveling around another

Read More

Bond, Peter. *DK Guide to Space*. New York: DK Publishing, 1999.

Couper, Heather, and Nigel Henbest. *DK Space Encyclopedia*. New York: DK Publishing, 1999.

Ridpath, Ian. *The Facts on File Atlas of Stars and Planets: A Beginner's Guide to the Universe*. New York: Facts on File, 1993.

Internet Sites

Astronomy.com
http://www.astronomy.com/home.asp

Windows to the Universe
http://windows.engin.umich.edu/

NASA: Just for Kids
http://www.nasa.gov/kids.html

The Nine Planets
http://seds.lpl.arizona.edu/nineplanets/nineplanets/